WRITERS REPUBLIC

Oath Keeper

RAYMOND GLEN POMPA

WRITERS REPUBLIC L.L.C.

515 Summit Ave. Unit R1
Union City, NJ 07087, USA

Website: **www.writersrepublic.com**
Hotline: **1-877-656-6838**
Email: **info@writersrepublic.com**

Ordering Information:
Quantity sales. Special discounts are available on quantity purchases by corporations, associations, and others. For details, contact the publisher at the address above.

Library of Congress Control Number:		2021944140	
ISBN-13:	978-1-63728-429-2	[Paperback Edition]	
	978-1-63728-430-8	[Digital Edition]	

Rev. date: 07/28/2021

Dedication

I fell in love with your grace. I will always love you.

Thank you for everything.

Juliette Zandrea Gallegos

Contents

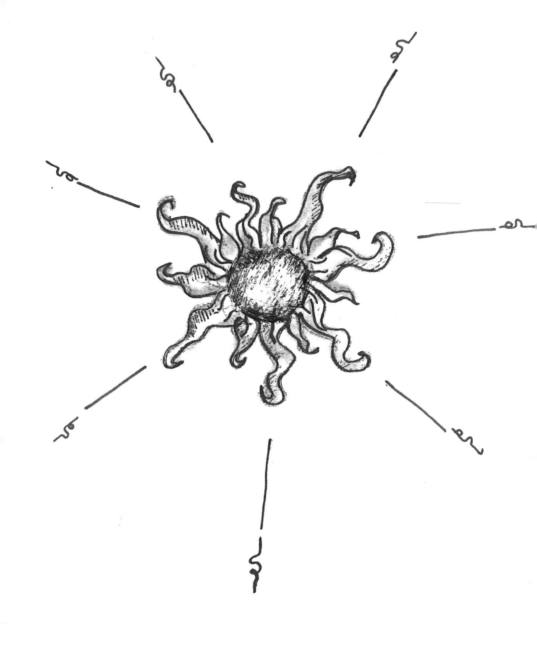

Chapter One: *The Sun*

Poem #1

A love that seems to last forever.

Reaching for her hand,

confused as to why life has brought us together,

but accepting the blessing of us.

She feels so soft and warm; she feels like home.

I can finally sleep through the night knowing my heart has found a home.

My first time realizing that my happiest place on earth is wherever
you are.

Falling in love, falling into the unknown.

Seeing my favorite person smile.

The broken road of heartache has finally become worth it.

Feeling a rush of energy from the touch of her lips,

and enjoying the thought of growing old with her.

Following your heart can be terrifying,

but she is by far the only person I will ever adore.

I want to love vitality into your life and light into your heart.

I have so many definitions of love, and she defines them all.

Nothing makes my heart smile quite like you do.

My life began when I met you.

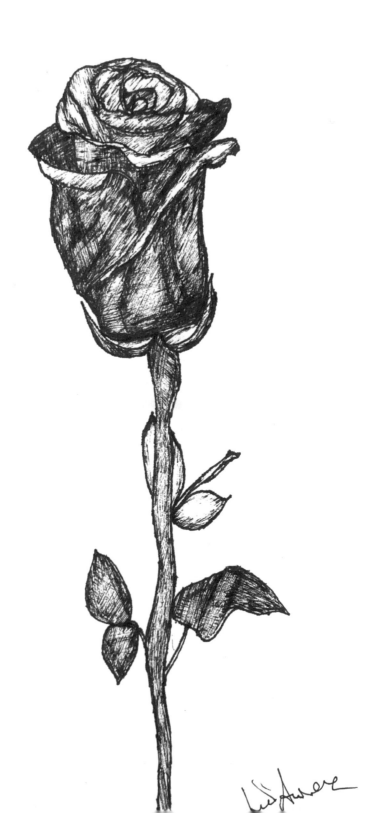

EveryThing

I want to learn about you, everything there is to know.

Everything that makes you sad, all the things that make you glow.

All the beauty in your heart, everything that makes your soul.

A friend in time, a friend of mine, you are not a trophy just for show.

You are a blessing in my life, and I will never let you go.

Rose-Colored Shades

I view the world through a shade of red, a world where some things are meant to be said.

Words like: I miss you, I need you, and I love you.

I wonder if you think of me

Or all the things that we could be

I find you in my memories

Genuine and ethereally

Here is something I would like for you to know

I would give you my heart and soul

All my love for you to have and hold

Since a heart like yours is made of gold

Yellow Rose

A yellow rose swaying slightly within the meadow.

A serene place where only love and hope grow.

Beautiful at first glance with an aura that I cannot resist.

Cautioned by past traumas, I move forward because my heart insists.

There is a soft breeze in the air, a warm wind that soothes my bare skin.

Feelings of peace and clarity wash away my sins.

With every step I take, I know that wherever she is,

is where I am meant to be.

Although her thorns are much sharper than most, I am sure this flower is meant for me.

I was meant to find her, and I thank God every day that she is mine.

Raymond Glen Pompa

Dear Mind,

Why do you fight against what I feel so much?

With love,

Heart

Dear Heart,

I am glad that you remember I exist! I do not mean to fight or resist what you feel. I only desire to protect what is left of the person we coexist within.

With logic,

Mind

She has always looked so good to me.

With her slender frame and soft brown skin.

Sparkling brown eyes that I get lost in.

Long hair that hangs gently down her shoulders.

She looks so good to me, and with every glance,

she knows it is my heart she has taken over.

Haven

In the moments when you find happiness is close
It is my arms I hope you long to be held by most
In the times you find sadness creeping into your bones
It is my heart I hope you will call home
Whether you are experiencing life's sorrow or joy, my dear
I hope you find a haven when I am near.

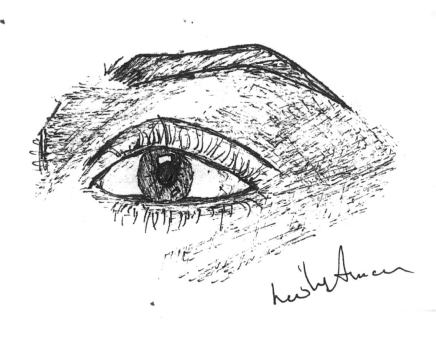

A beautiful, stubborn queen

Most adored

With my heart on my sleeve

Everlasting promises of heaven

Clouding judgement, Devil's embrace

Darkness invades.

In her kingdom

The euphoria and bliss of Nirvana

May become a reality.

Pluviophile

A pluviophile is a lover of rain,

but I am not quite sure I can use that word to describe myself.

I love when it rains because it reminds me of her and the night we met.

I felt joy and peace of mind when I was with her.

As the rain pours, my tears fall, but not from sadness. Soft tears of joy run down my cheeks as I reflect on how I felt in that moment. For a moment, I was happy.

I was happy with her and excited to see what the future had in store for us.

I would give anything to feel that way again.

The way I feel was set in stone.

A brilliant plan for a soul's aspiration and reincarnation,

Etched in fate by familiar blood and bones.

Fueled by desire and lustful temptation,

She is everything we have ever wanted.

The leading hand to our salvation,

Carved with precision through love and affection.

Two sides of the same coin,

promising protection.

In hopes that our intimate souls would one day rejoin,

long after we left this earth.

Long after my final hour.

Allow my affinity to be a testament to her worth

I want to take all her pain and store it inside of me,

her guardian angel's vessel fulfilling his purpose.

I want to wash her scars in an ocean of patience and understanding.

From a sea that calls to her,

Cancer's very own beach for connection.

I want to dry her skin with adoration.

Loving hands that touch her body delicately.

I want to keep her warm in an embrace of loyalty and love everlasting.

The sanctuary her heart desires,

I want to be her person.

A garden full of red roses,

the silver city of unconditional love at the tip of our noses.

These flowers fade like the life of a loved one with an illness.

Nothing beautiful ever stays and a day spent without loving her is another day that has been spent in waste.

They say it is better to never rush love but at the thought of you and me,

I make haste.

Heading to the garden, the place where unconditional love can soften the heart she has chosen to harden.

Making my way to the silver city... because I want to breathe again because I want to breathe life into my lungs once more.

An aroma that smells so sweet, an everlasting scent

I can breathe her in over and over again

I have always known this...

All I want is you.

The Sun

The sun will rise again.

As seen by the lover who reminisces on the broken bond between a cherished friend,

Symbolizing a new day in a world where the concept of time is meaningless.

Giving faith to the broken-hearted lover who lives with too much kindness.

The sun shines brightly and reaches the darkest corner of the world.

Much like the smile of a giraffe loving lovely girl

To remind us that we cannot hide from who we truly are,

Shaped into existence by our past.

Molded by memories and scars,

For a decision only oneself can make;

To live a life of fear or faith.

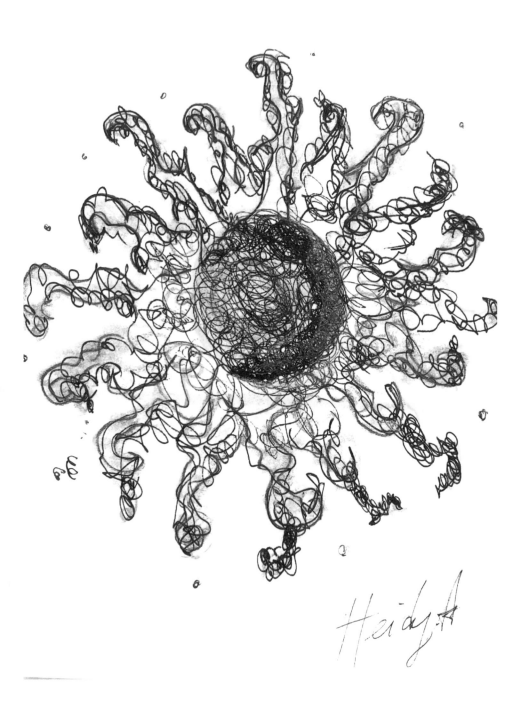

Raymond Glen Pompa

Chapter Two: *The Moon*

Poem #2

Planning for forever,

Without really knowing any better,

hoping lessons taught by life thus far would succeed at keeping us afloat.

So sad to see the keeper of your heart leave.

Making plans for a future together,

full of all the things that make life worth living.

Seeing her walk away from everything.

Tears falling like the rain,

Sound of pain-filled shallow breaths,

the breaking of one's heart.

The bittersweet feeling of everything that could have been,

hoping she does not leave me in her memories.

The Thought of You

At the thought of you, I unravel

Bringing down my walls and insecurities

Exposing my vulnerabilities

I am more afraid than I have ever been at the thought of not seeing you
again

One half of me in this world, and I cannot fill the hole like before.

The thought of you and I,

how I would give, anything to feel whole once more.

Heidy.A

If only our love story would blossom with the seeds planted by our hearts, then maybe she would stay.

However, our half-written story may be on its last chapter as the petals of love quickly begin to wither away.

The keeper of my heart,

where have you gone as my world falls apart?

She is not hard to love.

It truly breaks my heart to know she feels that way.

Would you like my honest opinion?

The only thing difficult about her and love is not being loved by her.

Achromatic

For a moment, there was color in my world again. Saturated by the beauty of you. And when you decided it was your time to go... the sky returned to its shade of gray.

There is a difference between falling in love and giving your heart away.

Suffering

Within my broken heart, I will find a fraction of clarity

Yearning for my own peace of mind along with her sincerity

Holding onto memories of us and dreams anew

I find myself searching for pieces of me within the remnants of you

And it hurts me down to my very core

An ache in my skin and bones I have never felt before

Love's Sorrow

I long for a better tomorrow.

A tomorrow where the sensation of loneliness does not

ache like a merciless pain.

Coursing through my veins,

Filling my bone and marrow with remorse,

Happiness and sadness birthed by an elegant source.

Mind,

We want the same thing! She brings new faith into our old soul.

Follow my intuition, and we will not fail!

Truly yours,

Heart

Heart,

You are still the same fool you have always been, recklessly guided by your emotions and loving everyone else without leaving any love for yourself. Do you not grow weary of this?

Yours truly,

Mind

My Darkness

From the age of seven, there has been a shadowy figure standing at seven feet tall attached to me.

He laughs when I cry and wants nothing more than for me to take my own life. He grins sinisterly when I am happy, knowing he will find a way to seduce my energy and give all that he is to shape me into an empty vessel.

The Hopeful Heart

I should not have said goodbye, but what other choice did I have?

Whether I chose to leave or to stay the fact that you did not feel the same anymore is difficult to live with.

I have been through that before, loving someone unconditionally, loving someone more than myself. Knowing they would never see me in the same light.

For now, I must accept the way things are.

Even though I chose to say goodbye, you will always have a place in my heart and mind.

That is why I say a prayer for you every chance I get. Please do not forget about me...

And God...

If there are any miracles you have in store for me, please bring us back together again.

Her

Her body is like a work of art; each tattoo tells me a little more about her life.

Her smile gives me faith, and I have known from the start.

I had every intention of keeping her around.

Logically it is too soon to tell, but she has a way about her that picks me up when I am feeling down.

Yeah... yeah... I know I have been rushing in a lot lately.

But the clock is ticking, and I put the cuckoo in crazy...

Loving her is the only thing that makes sense in my madness.

From Me To You

From the darkness, a new light surfaced.

You gave my life meaning when it lacked purpose.

I found forever in your delicate brown eyes.

Your essence has inspired me to rise.

Your grace has influenced me to grow.

The gift of life from the yellow rose.

I have found someone worthy of my love, and that someone is you.

Still, the words that I need to hear most is," I Love You too."

I felt like I could take on the world when I was with you.

The beginning of the end was near, and I had no clue.

Venturing into the unknown with your hand in mine.

Allowing my life to fade away as if I had time.

Now that you are gone, I feel more lost than ever.

I was told that with time I would feel better.

However, no one has a clue how I feel when the night falls, and the little voice in my head calls out to me.

If I really wanted to end it all, I could use a gun or some pills or smash my head into things until the blood spills.

When the night comes, and I have nowhere to run and no place to hide.

Hello, says the darkness that was hidden inside the boy who once thought he could take on the world.

He held himself together through thick and thin, twenty-three years of life that have never really been good to him.

He was doing so well...

If one would say well is the same as crying himself to sleep and wearing a smile on his face at times when he felt weak.

The façade of happiness, he wore so well until the day when he no longer has the energy to fake it.

Until the day when he realizes he has nothing left in him to make it.

He wore it so well, he hid it so well, but all that effort just to shatter in the end.

Raymond Glen Pompa

All for that one regret that reminds him of who he truly is.

The only regret that haunts him to this day...

How I had your heart in my hands and let it slip away

I could die today...

And no one would care, not even you.

Since you cut all ties except for the red string attached to my soul.

Allowing all the darkness, he was holding back to seep out of a forsaken hole.

In my heart, I could die today... but the truth is when one loses faith, they are already dead.

Ray's Sake

Dear brother, can you hear me?

brother, can you hear me...

I miss you dearly.

Tell the Lord I have tried my best.

My tired heart and soul longs for rest.

I will always miss the days when we used to laugh and play.

Imagination flowing into our everyday life without a care in the world.

Laughing, crying, and playing the way that children do.

Dear lover, why do you fear me?

lover, why do you fear me...

I miss you, darling.

Tell the Lord this feeling is nothing new.

I will always think of you.

In skies of gray and nights of blue,

I hope someday we meet again so that our bond may bloom.

Welcoming each other with forgiveness and open arms.

Smiling at our wittiness and delightful charm.

Finding joy and content in each other's hearts.

All I can ask is why... Why do you not love me?

The Moon

The moon returns to take her place

Glistening off the lover's tearful face

Symbolizing the day's end

A reminder that the sun will always rise again

The moonlight glows, yet the lovers have gone to a place that no one
knows

Never to be heard from or seen again

The darkest corner of the world

A place where some may never return

With agony that endlessly burns

From the lesson, the lover never learned.

To love yourself before loving someone else, to protect your heart because
it is the only one you have, and if you do not cherish it, then who will...

Chapter Three: *The Truth*

Poem #3

Wandering souls traveling through time,

the only worlds that matter to me,

is yours and mine.

Searching for common ground,

Why do you mean so much to me?

One amazing girl with such a

unique personality,

Being lucky enough to have your eyes, if only for a moment.

I wanted to have unforgettable laughs with you,

Be your shoulder to cry on,

someone who can always be there for you,

your friend, your lover, someone like no other,

and most importantly,

someone who loves you even at your worst.

I thank God every day for bringing you into my life.

Knowing that if we stayed together, there is no reality we cannot create.

She is the most stubborn girl I have ever met, and she has every right to be that way.

There comes a time when she can be stubborn to a fault, but she does it to protect herself.

You will always mean the world to me...because of that,

I really hope you find your happiness in life, in love,

and in everything, you set your heart on.

I want you to realize how beautiful you truly are and understand,

how much better the world is with you in it.

You will achieve so many great things,

and the person you are becoming is nothing to be ashamed of.

In fact, you should be proud of who you are.

Please do not be so hard on yourself.

Someone as wonderful as you deserve the world.

The door to my heart and soul has been unlocked.

The hinges that were believed to be sealed shut were opened by someone many would call beautiful

but would never understand just how much she brings meaning to that word.

The door remains unsecured,

and I wait patiently for the day she decides to walk through it.

So that we may experience a love that neither of us has known before.

Our hearts will forever remain connected, and I will love you always.

Mind,

Everything we wanted has finally come to pass. Thank you for believing in her. Your faith made all the difference. Being a fool has led us to a new beginning;

a beginning where we all find peace, love, and happiness.

Take care,

Heart

Heart,

The love they share is far from ordinary. I may not understand it entirely, but he is happy, and I can think clearly now. She truly does bring out the best in him. I applaud your persistence. It seems that dreams do come true, and you are still a fool, but a fool with good intentions.

Sincerely,

Mind

February 14, 2019

In February, I met someone great. Do not get me wrong, she was not perfect, but she was perfect for me. I could hardly take my eyes off the woman before me with big brown eyes and hair that fell swiftly down her shoulders. Later into the night, I realized it was probably better to take our conversation elsewhere since the topics were getting deeper. Sitting in my car, we talked about each other. It is a faint memory now, be that as it may, I will never truly forget it or her. I did not want to leave that night. After hours of talking, she decided it was time to go. I got out of the car to give her a hug in the pouring rain. During this embrace, she sneaked in a kiss catching me completely off guard. Her smile and chuckle that came quickly afterward as she walked away still make me smile as I think about it. I wish I could be with the girl who kissed me that night. Every time it rains, I am reminded of her.

Sunset With You

I knew I had to see her again and soon. Luckily, I was able to pick her up a few days later for us to take a stroll along Mission Beach together. I find myself going there often, mostly because I love being near water. I do not know if I go there to relive our memory or escape from it at this point. All I do know is that walking alongside her made me feel whole again. I remember watching her and contemplating spending the rest of my life with her. Asking myself if she is really someone, I can call my person. I came to the conclusion that if it were so, then I would be a lucky guy. For the first time, I really enjoyed watching the sunset. The gleam from the sky illuminated the ocean, and just as sure as the sun sets, I was certain there was more to her and me. At the time, I did not realize that meant so many lessons filled with joy and sadness.

The Best Birthday

We made love on my birthday, and I consider that the best gift she could have given me. It is a connection during a time where disconnection was becoming a normalized idea within my mind. I listened to her heartbeat afterward, and to this day, I still consider it my favorite melody. I tend to say too much, so when I told her that I finally felt like the hole in my heart was being filled, I have no idea how she took that, but I spoke my heart's truth and what was said is still evident to this day.

For the past two years, I have been searching for answers. The day we met, she set my heart aflame, and I have been doing all that I can to protect the embers from the cold winter that has embraced my life as the fire slowly burns out.

While on this journey, I have looked to God and to a dear friend of mine. This spiritualist has guided me through dark times and reminds me every chance she gets that Juliette and I are meant to be together.

Through my friend's prayer and meditation, I will have my salvation. She believes the only future that exists is one where you and I belong together. She believes there is something we need to complete in our lives and within each other.

You make my heart so happy sometimes it hurts. Clenching my chest as if I can hold in the love that is born from your grace. Bursting with joy, my tears begin to fall, and all the sadness I felt is no more.

No one ever notices how beautiful a broken heart can be when the person you adore is much more than ordinary. The idea of building and growing with someone you admire can be quite scary. To trust someone with your intimacy, sacred truths, and scars. Do not be afraid, my dear, for I am your haven from the darkness that clings to you. Within your fears lies doubt, but beyond the doubt lies our new beginning and happy ending.

Self-love will always be a priority...

But if you are lucky enough to have someone

That means the world to you

Treat them with genuine love and kindness.

I think about her every second of my entire day. I fall asleep, hoping she will suddenly change her mind about us. I cling to the idea of us being together because it is the only dream I have left in my heart. I have fought tooth and nail for us to be together, in the physical realm and in the spiritual realm.

I wanted us to grow together like no other. Raise a family together and purchase our first home together. Have children that act like me and look like you or vice versa. I would fall in love all over again with a mini version of you. My purpose would be fulfilled if only I were to spend the rest of my life with you.

Know that you are not alone, my darling. I will pray for you every chance I get. Please allow the people who care for you to be there for you in your moments of weakness. There is a reason why you are still here. Before, when you chose to give up, understand that it was not your time to go. God has so much in store for you.

Watching you try to take on the world all by yourself hurts me too, you know? This life is not meant to be lived alone. We need our friends and family to lift us up when all hope is lost. I want to protect you at all costs. I want to be your guardian angel.

You make me feel simple and clean.

"Why do you love her?"

"Because she is imperfect, and all of her flaws make you realize how beautiful imperfection truly is."

You are my reason for living.

I understand how that can be quite a burden to carry.

Should you let me be the one to love you, then I shall lighten the heaviness on your heart.

You mean the world to me.

I hope you understand that I had to cross the boundaries and lines between us. I needed to wake you up. I fought for us every day, and even with all my time, tears, and effort, I could not convince you to stay. I do not regret doing so. I had to call you out on your bullshit so you could see how destructive your behavior had become. You were killing something that I loved more than life itself. I could not watch you kill yourself anymore. I loved you, and I fought with you every day to prove it in hopes that you would see yourself and the world differently. Hopefully, in a similar light that I once saw you in, a loving light, you could reach even the darkest corner of the world.

The Truth

I love you more than you may ever comprehend. No one else will ever take the place in my heart that I have reserved for you. I will always wait for you.

Juju's Love

Freedom...

The only person who can save me from me...

Oath Keeper

I will never understand why I allowed myself to love someone like you. You were never any good to me. I reflect on the memories we made, and it hurts when I realize you have always treated me as less than a friend.

I hope we never meet again. I hope I never see you again. I would love to say that I do not harbor any negative feelings towards you, but the truth is I hate you—someone, I once loved with all my heart and soul and would have given the world to. The oath I made to God was that I would always love you. An oath that I can no longer keep because if I do, it will lead me down a destructive path of loneliness and isolation.

Whenever I close my eyes and visualize us together, all that I see is me standing in a vast space full of darkness. The thought of being in the darkness does not frighten me; however, the scariest part is how I am willing to stay there. This was love at one point. Pure and genuine love for you.

However, the loneliness I have felt and the darkness I have faced for us with you not being here for me has transformed into hate. May you read these words and fully come to understand that you let go of someone who loved you unconditionally.

Thank you for not loving me. I would have spent a lifetime in the cage I was desperate to escape from. I would have spent my entire life loving the wrong person.

I am sorry, God, that I made such a promise to you, an oath that I could not keep.

Raymond Glen Pompa

Author's bio: Raymond Glen Pompa

Raymond Pompa was born and raised in Tulare, California. Upon graduation from Tulare Union High School, he served in the United States Marine Corps. When Raymond served in the military he spent most of his service in San Diego, California. At the end of his service he began working as a police officer. When Raymond isn't working, he enjoys spending time with his family and loved ones, playing basketball, and writing poetry.

Illustrator's bio: Heidy Alice Albavera

Growing up, believe it or not I never had the thought to do art. I was afraid to speak up or take initiative, let alone try to learn new things. My family was chaotic and I moved around a lot so I mostly kept to myself. Art pulled me out of that and I bloomed so beautifully.

We all have our story and my story really built me into the person I am today. The feeling of just being able to create anything I want is so mystical to me. I was 20 years old when I fell deeply in love with something other than a person. I see the world differently now and I pay attention to every detail on earth whether it's a: nice sliced melon, a family walking, the sky, a lizard on my patio, or the city lights, all I see is art.

You can say I'm a very joyful and a goofy creative artist. I love to express my happiness and put it onto a nice blank canvas. I set the mood, play some good music, dance it out, and feel my body creating every mark. I love to do expressionism art, abstract, surrealism art, pretty much whatever I feel like. I love mistakes; it helps me personally with my creativeness. My motto is mistakes breed greatness. I like all mediums, but the one that intrigues me the most is acrylic paint. I get lost in the harmony of mixing colors and creating a perfect blend. The people that influenced me during my art journey are my buddies Sean, Olivia, and Lucie. Sean is my best friend and also an amazing artist, I wouldn't be the artist I am today if it weren't for him. I'm Lucie and Olivia's nanny, and they taught me my passion in teaching others art. I love everything that art brings. Joy, memories, love, adrenaline, just pure bliss. I'm very proud of the person I am today. I am pursuing my dreams and I can't wait to see what's next.

CPSIA information can be obtained
at www.ICGtesting.com
Printed in the USA
LVHW070926170821
695403LV00001BA/43